MUSICAL MOMENTS

Alto Saxophone

Book 3

12 original compositions
& arrangements
for Alto Saxophone & Piano

Selected and edited by
Kirsty Hetherington

Published by
Trinity College London Press Ltd
trinitycollege.com

Registered in England
Company no. 09726123

Copyright © 2011 Trinity College London
Fifth impression, January 2024

Unauthorised photocopying is illegal
No part of this publication may be copied or reproduced in any
form or by any means without the prior permission of the publisher.

Layout: Scott Barnard

Printed in England by Caligraving Ltd

Let Them Sing

Jeffrey Wilson
(born 1957)

Bourrée

from *Music for the Royal Fireworks* HWV 351

arr. Robin Hagues

George Frideric Handel
(1685-1759)

Copyright © 2011 Trinity College London

Grand Parade
from *Scenes of Childhood* op. 62

arr. John DeHolt

Theodor Kullak
(1818–1882)

Danse Arabe
from *The Nutcracker Suite*

arr. Robin Hagues

Pyotr Ilyich Tchaikovsky
(1840–1893)

Danse Arabe = Arabian Dance

Heatwave

Andy Scott
(born 1966)

Night at a Round Table

Chris Gumbley
(born 1958)

TRINITY
COLLEGE LONDON PRESS

MUSICAL MOMENTS

Alto Saxophone

Book 3

12 original compositions
& arrangements
for Alto Saxophone & Piano

Selected and edited by
Kirsty Hetherington

Piano accompaniment

Contents

Wilson	Let Them Sing	4
Handel	Bourrée (from *Music for the Royal Fireworks* HWV 351)	6
Kullak	Grand Parade (from *Scenes from Childhood* op. 62)	8
Tchaikovsky	Danse Arabe (from *The Nutcracker Suite*)	10
Scott	Heatwave	12
Gumbley	Night at a Round Table	15
Mozart	Minuet and Trio (from *Viennese Sonata*)	18
Mower	Light in Shade	20
Buckland	Paper Boats	22
Gossec	Gavotte	24
Street	Dancing in my Dreams	26
Bonfá	Gentle Rain	28

Published by
Trinity College London Press Ltd
trinitycollege.com

Registered in England
Company no. 09726123

Copyright © 2011 Trinity College London
Fifth impression, January 2024

Unauthorised photocopying is illegal
No part of this publication may be copied or reproduced in any
form or by any means without the prior permission of the publisher.

Layout: Scott Barnard

Printed in England by Caligraving Ltd

Let Them Sing

Jeffrey Wilson
(born 1957)

Bourrée

from *Music for the Royal Fireworks* HWV 351

arr. Robin Hagues

George Frideric Handel
(1685-1759)

Grand Parade

from *Scenes of Childhood* op. 62

arr. John DeHolt

Theodor Kullak
(1818-1882)

Danse Arabe
from *The Nutcracker Suite*

arr. Robin Hagues

Pyotr Ilyich Tchaikovsky
(1840-1893)

Danse Arabe = Arabian Dance

Heatwave

Andy Scott
(born 1966)

Night at a Round Table

Chris Gumbley
(born 1958)

Minuet and Trio

from *Viennese Sonata*

arr. John DeHolt

Wolfgang Amadeus Mozart
(1756-1791)

Light in Shade

Mike Mower
(born 1958)

Paper Boats

Rob Buckland
(born 1967)

Gavotte

arr. Andrew Challinger

François-Joseph Gossec
(1734-1829)

Dancing in my Dreams

Karen Street
(born 1959)

Gentle Rain

arr. Andreas Panayi

Luiz Floriano Bonfá
(1922-2001)

Music by LUIZ BONFÁ. Lyrics by MATT DUBEY. © 1965 EMI UNART CATALOG INC.
Exclusive Worldwide Print Rights administered by ALFRED MUSIC PUBLISHING CO., INC.
All Rights Reserved. Used by Permission.

Minuet and Trio

from *Viennese Sonata*

arr. John DeHolt

Wolfgang Amadeus Mozart
(1756-1791)

Light in Shade

Mike Mower
(born 1958)

Paper Boats

Rob Buckland
(born 1967)

Gavotte

arr. Andrew Challinger

François-Joseph Gossec
(1734–1829)

Dancing in my Dreams

Karen Street
(born 1959)

Gentle Rain

arr. Andreas Panayi

Luiz Floriano Bonfá
(1922–2001)